THE NBA FINALS

BY ALLAN MOREY

TORQUE
TM

BELLWETHER MEDIA · MINNEAPOLIS, MN

TM

Are you ready to take it to the extreme? Torque books thrust you into the action-packed world of sports, vehicles, mystery, and adventure. These books may include dirt, smoke, fire, and chilling tales. **WARNING**: read at your own risk.

This edition first published in 2019 by Bellwether Media, Inc.

No part of this publication may be reproduced in whole or in part without written permission of the publisher. For information regarding permission, write to Bellwether Media, Inc., Attention: Permissions Department, 6012 Blue Circle Drive, Minnetonka, MN 55343.

Library of Congress Cataloging-in-Publication Data

Names: Morey, Allan, author.
Title: The NBA Finals / by Allan Morey.
Description: Minneapolis, Minnesota : Bellwether Media, Inc., 2019. | Series:
   Torque: Sports Championships | Includes bibliographical references and
   index. | Audience: Grades: 3-7. | Audience: Ages: 7-12.
Identifiers: LCCN 2018001800 (print) | LCCN 2018004277 (ebook) | ISBN
   9781626178649 (hardcover : alk. paper) | ISBN 9781681036052 (ebook)
   | ISBN 9781618914842 (paperback : alk. paper)
Subjects: LCSH: National Basketball Association–History–Juvenile
   literature. | Basketball–Tournaments–United States–History–Juvenile
   literature.
Classification: LCC GV885.515.N37 (ebook) | LCC GV885.515.N37 M67 2019
   (print) | DDC 796.323/64–dc23
LC record available at https://lccn.loc.gov/2018001800

Editor: Rebecca Sabelko   Designer: Jon Eppard

Printed in the United States of America, North Mankato, MN.

TABLE OF CONTENTS

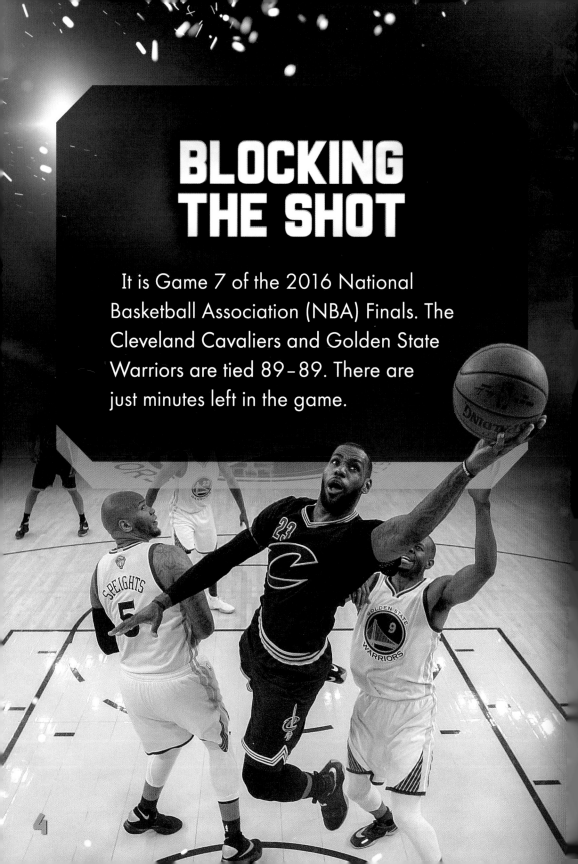

BLOCKING THE SHOT

It is Game 7 of the 2016 National Basketball Association (NBA) Finals. The Cleveland Cavaliers and Golden State Warriors are tied 89–89. There are just minutes left in the game.

ANDRE IGUODALA

LEBRON JAMES

Warriors' Andre Iguodala goes up for an easy **layup**. Out of nowhere, Cavaliers' LeBron James jumps to block the shot. James keeps the Warriors from scoring! Cleveland goes on to win 93–89. They are NBA champs!

WHAT ARE THE NBA FINALS?

The NBA Finals are a series of games that decide the NBA champion. They are played at the end of every basketball season. The series starts in late spring.

The NBA Finals are a best-of-seven
series. The first team to win four games
is the champion.

The winner of the NBA Finals receives the Larry O'Brien NBA Championship Trophy. O'Brien served as **commissioner** from 1975 to 1984. He helped the NBA expand.

LARRY O'BRIEN ·······▶
NBA CHAMPIONSHIP
TROPHY

8

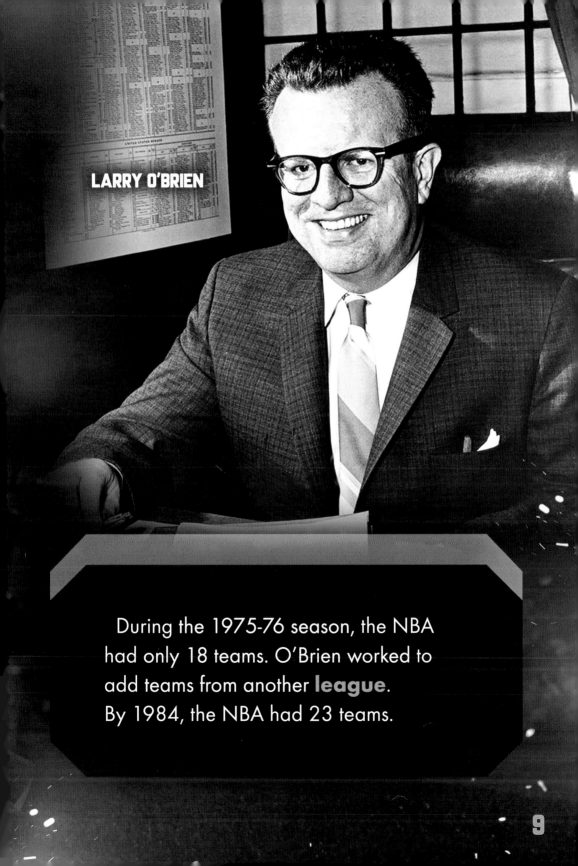

LARRY O'BRIEN

During the 1975-76 season, the NBA had only 18 teams. O'Brien worked to add teams from another **league**. By 1984, the NBA had 23 teams.

HISTORY OF THE NBA FINALS

There used to be two basketball leagues. The National Basketball League (NBL) began in 1937. It had 13 teams. The Basketball Association of America (BAA) started in 1946 with 11 teams.

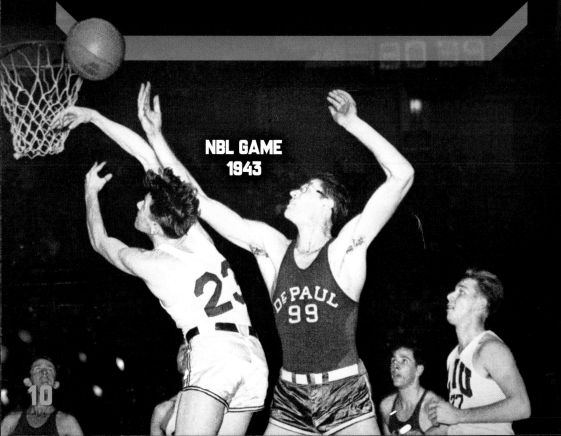

NBL GAME
1943

**BAA GAME
1947**

The BAA played a major role in
the beginnings of the NBA. Its first
championship teams are considered
the first NBA champions.

From the start, the NBL and BAA struggled. The two leagues competed for fans and players. Some teams even switched from one league to the other. Teams in both leagues had a hard time making money.

In 1949, the NBL joined the BAA. They formed the NBA. The new league had 17 teams.

GOING WAY BACK

Five current NBA teams can trace their roots back to the NBL. They are the Atlanta Hawks, Detroit Pistons, Los Angeles Lakers, Philadelphia 76ers, and Sacramento Kings.

NBA FINALS CHAMPS

THE BOSTON CELTICS

1957, 1959, 1960, 1961, 1962, 1963, 1964, 1965, 1966, 1968, 1969, 1974, 1976, 1981, 1984, 1986, 2008

NBA MVP

Bill Russell played for the Boston Celtics from 1959 to 1969. During his career, his defensive skills helped the Celtics win 11 NBA Finals.

BILL RUSSELL

ROAD TO THE NBA FINALS

The NBA has two **conferences**. They are the Eastern and the Western Conferences. Each is divided into three **divisions** of 5 teams.

BEST RECORD

The Golden State Warriors won 73 games during the 2015-16 season! They hold the record for most wins in a single season.

NBA teams play 82 games in a season. The teams are ranked by their win-loss records. The 8 best teams in each conference make it to the **playoffs**.

There are three rounds of the NBA playoffs. Teams compete in a series of seven games during each round.

In each division, 8 teams play in the first round. The 4 winning teams move on to the Conference **Semifinals**. After that, the remaining teams play in the Conference Finals. The winners of these games meet in the NBA Finals.

NBA FINALS BRACKET

WEST
CONFERENCE

FIRST ROUND SEMIFINALS CONFERENCE FINALS NBA FINALS

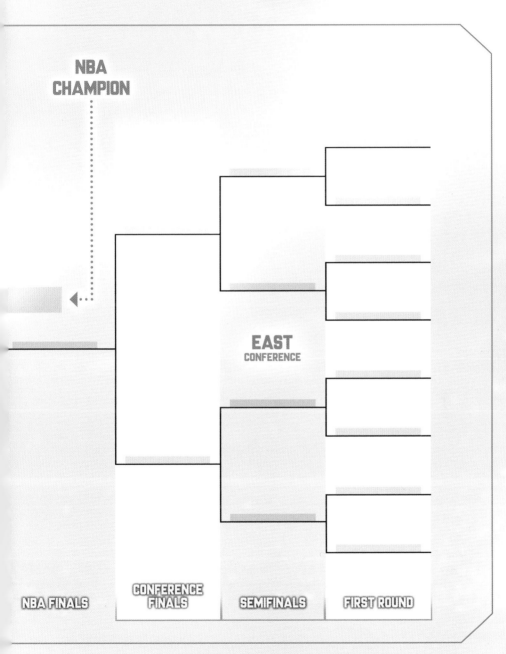

NBA
CHAMPION

EAST
CONFERENCE

NBA FINALS | CONFERENCE FINALS | SEMIFINALS | FIRST ROUND

SITTING COURTSIDE

Many people think the best seats at a basketball game are along the side of the court. Courtside seats are just feet away from the action!

During the NBA Finals, celebrities fill up courtside seats. They include music stars, actors, and even politicians. Seeing who is at the game is one more reason to check out the NBA Finals!

GLOSSARY

commissioner–an official in charge of overseeing a professional sport league

conferences–large groupings of sports teams that often play each other

divisions–small groupings of sports teams; there are usually several divisions of teams in a conference.

layup–a shot made near the basket often by bouncing the ball off the backboard

league–a large group of sports teams that often play each other

playoffs–games played after the regular season is over; playoff games determine which teams play in the NBA Finals.

semifinals–games played right before the final game in a tournament

TO LEARN MORE

AT THE LIBRARY

Chandler, Matt. *The Science of Basketball: The Top Ten Ways Science Affects the Game*. North Mankato, Minn.: Capstone, 2016.

Clausen-Grace, Nicki, and Jeff Grace. *Basketball Superstars*. Mankato, Minn.: Black Rabbit Books, 2018.

Mikoley, Kate. *Basketball: Stats, Facts, and Figures*. New York, N.Y.: Gareth Stevens Publishing, 2018.

ON THE WEB

Learning more about the NBA Finals is as easy as 1, 2, 3.

1. Go to www.factsurfer.com.

2. Enter "NBA Finals" into the search box.

3. Click the "Surf" button and you will see a list of related web sites.

With factsurfer.com, finding more information is just a click away.

INDEX